How to Homeschool 9th and 10th Grade

Simple Steps for Starting Strong

Lee Binz,
The HomeScholar

First Printing, 2014

Printed in the United States of America

ISBN: 1500512125
ISBN-13: 978-1500512125

Disclaimer: Parents assume full responsibility for the education of their children in accordance with state law. College requirements vary, so make sure to check with the colleges about specific requirements for homeschoolers. We offer no guarantees, written or implied, that the use of our products and services will result in college admissions or scholarship awards.

How to Homeschool 9th and 10th Grade

Simple Steps for Starting Strong

What are Coffee Break Books?

"How to Homeschool 9th and 10th Grade" is part of The HomeScholar's Coffee Break Book series.

Designed especially for parents who don't want to spend hours and hours reading a 400-page book on homeschooling high school, each book combines Lee's practical and friendly approach with detailed, but easy-to-digest information, perfect to read over a cup of coffee at your favorite coffee shop!

Never overwhelming, always accessible and manageable, each book in the series will give parents the tools they need to tackle the tasks of homeschooling high school, one warm sip at a time.

Everything about these Coffee Break Books is designed to suggest simplicity, ease and comfort; from the size (fits in a purse), to the font and paragraph length (easy on the eyes), to the price (the same as a Starbucks Venti Triple Caramel Macchiato). Unlike a fancy coffee drink, however, these books are guilt-free pleasures you will want to enjoy again and again!

Table of Contents

How to Homeschool 9th and 10th Grade

Introduction

Guidance Counselors, Teachers, and Mentors

When you enter the high school years, it's time for you to be your child's guidance counselor, and help guide them into college and career. And guess what? You are the absolute best guidance counselor for your child! Nobody loves them and knows them as well as you do. Nobody cares more than you about what happens to your child! The love you have for your child will ensure success.

Guidance Counselor Basics

To be a successful guidance counselor, make sure that your child is working at their level in every subject all the time in high school. You don't want to force your child into calculus when they're in 9th grade because they need calculus by the time they graduate. Instead, have them work at their own level in math.

Don't rush things. You don't want to throw a higher-level math course at them so early that they end up with no understanding of the basics. You want to give your child the best quality education and ensure they come out of your homeschool high school an educated young person, prepared for college and life.

Keep in mind that teenagers are notorious for changing their minds! You just never know what they're going to come up with from moment to moment. One day they want to be the next Bill Gates and the next they might want to be a football star.

Ensure your child is well prepared for college. If they decide to go to college, they'll be ready to go. If they don't go to college, you have provided a wonderful education for a well-rounded young adult. If they change their minds, as teenagers do, and decide to go to college again, they'll be ready!

I have included much more about your role as "high school guidance counselor" in Appendix 1.

Changing Role of Parents

Freshman year is your child's 9th grade year. In most locations, it's the first year of high school. It begins when a child is about 14 or 15 years old. This year is a good time to start thinking about college. Sophomore year is your child's 10th grade year. It starts when a child is about 15 or 16 years old. This is the time to start focusing on college prep!

Freshman and sophomore years are the transition years. You start to transition away from the teacher role you've become familiar with. Your role changes to the mentor, project manager or supervisor. You no longer teach, but supervise learning.

It can feel uncomfortable and it was a difficult transition for me, too! As a homeschool mom or dad, you get so used to being the teacher! You enter high school, terrified that you have to teach physics, calculus, or chemistry. However, when you homeschool a freshman or sophomore, you start to move away from being a teacher and begin guiding your child to start teaching themselves. You are now the mentor, encouraging them to learn physics or calculus. You are not so much teaching as you are facilitating, making sure they have the proper materials so they can learn on their own.

Because of this change, you may feel insecure when you first utilize self-teaching materials or math DVDs. You're not a failure if you can't teach algebra. When you start using a self-teaching video or have your child read the textbook on their own, that's actually a sign of success. You're doing it right! The ability to teach yourself is a lifelong skill that every college student and every employee needs to master. Adults teach themselves all the time. Successful adults don't wait for someone to spoon-feed them the information they need; they go out and get it. This transition from the student being the receiver of instruction to the seeker of an education is crucial for their long-term success and happiness.

Chapter 1

Priorities

Set your priorities in freshman and sophomore year. Consider what you have to do in order to be ready for college even if you aren't planning on college, just in case your child chooses to go. As you read this book, I will give you priorities in order from most important to those that are extra credit.

Know your local homeschool laws and how they apply to homeschooling high school. When you look at homeschool laws, they are not usually the same laws that apply to public schools. In most states, the law will detail what applies to public schools, what applies to private schools, and what applies to homeschool separately.

When the local news airs a report about how high school requires 100 hours of community service and a technology class, it probably does not apply to you as a homeschooler. You may choose to cover these, but it's probably not a homeschool requirement. Homeschool requirements are found in your state's homeschool law. Don't panic over the local high school graduation requirements; get acquainted with your local homeschool law here:

www.TheHomeScholar.com/know-your-state-homeschool-law.php

As you start homeschooling 9th and 10th grade, you are learning how to homeschool high school. Take it one step at a time. Keep good records, right from the start. Everything you keep is part of your child's official, lasting record.

Start looking ahead to college and understand that college preparation usually involves more than what is required for public high school graduation. By providing college prep to your child, you will be exceeding public high school requirements. Looking ahead to college is going to give you a better-educated child.

Chapter 2

Cover the Core

It's so important to cover those core classes in your homeschool. Your child will learn more when you work at their ability level than if they're getting frustrated by being pushed too quickly or bored because the work is too easy. If your child is ahead, push and encourage them to their ability level. Even if they're behind, you still need to make sure you're teaching at their ability level.

These next three chapters are a quick review of what is considered core for the high school years, as well as typical college expectations. For more detailed coverage of this topic, see my Coffee Break Book, "Planning High School

Courses: Charting the Course Toward High School Graduation."

English

English is important whether you're looking at high school graduation requirements or college requirements. You want your child to learn to read and write according to their ability level and you must cover four years of English. Make sure you cover English every year and that you include both reading and writing. An hour or more per day for five days a week most of the school year will earn your child one high school credit.

Math

Four years of math is also required. There is a standard progression that usually goes in this order: Pre-Algebra, Algebra 1, Geometry, Algebra 2, then either Trigonometry or Pre-Calculus. Advanced students may take Calculus as well. As a homeschool parent, your goal is to try to complete one math level per year.

Make sure your child does a math lesson every day. Math is not something you can skip. You may not have your child complete every problem in the book but make sure that a whole math lesson is done each day. That's how to get through one complete level a year even if you have a struggling learner who is working on 8th grade math during 9th grade.

If your child starts high school and takes a general mathematics course in 9th grade and then Pre-Algebra in 10th grade, it's still more important that they understand the core concepts so they can do as well as possible on high school tests than be pushed along too quickly. If they have a thorough understanding of Algebra 1, they'll do better on the SAT than if they are pushed through math regardless of their level.

Social Studies

Consider your child's learning style when teaching social studies. Some kids are prolific readers and using a literature-based curriculum may be a good choice for them. Children who are not good readers may need to be read to, listen to audiobooks, or watch videos in order to learn.

American History and World History are often considered the cornerstone classes of social studies, to be covered first in 9th grade and then built on in future years. American government and economics are generally taught later, in junior or senior year.

Science

When you get into high school, your child is ready to take on more rigorous academic work, such as from a high school text. In middle school, focus on nurturing your child's love of science. When they start 9th grade, they will already enjoy science and you can easily teach it as a rigorous high school academic class. Having that desire to learn science is all you need to begin teaching high school science.

Biology can be the first high school level science class you teach. I recommend starting science with biology and a lab in

9th grade. Enjoy hands-on experiments and delight directed learning labs to make science fun. Unit studies can encourage the love of learning in your child.

I encourage you to fearlessly forge ahead in math and science. It can be a little intimidating but there's no need to panic. By the time your child gets to the calculus or physics level, they will primarily be teaching themselves!

Chapter 3

Beyond the Basics

While prioritizing the core classes, look beyond the basics. Foreign language is often a requirement for high school graduation and colleges may require 2 to 4 years of a single foreign language. In other words, they don't want to see 1 year of Hebrew, 1 year of Latin, and 1 year of Greek. Instead, they want to see a big, solid chunk of a single foreign language.

Latin is a great language to study. It is a terrific jumping off point for learning the romance languages such as French or Italian. I taught my own children Latin starting in middle school, and we found it extremely helpful when we started learning high school French. However, you don't need Latin in order to start learning a foreign language.

Since colleges want to see 2 to 4 years of a single foreign language in high school, start during freshman year if possible. You really need to start that foreign language by the time your child is a sophomore to get in the minimum 2 or 3 years. If you studied a foreign language with your child in middle school and you used a high school level curriculum, you can get a head start and put those credits on your high school transcript as "Early High School Credits."

When I homeschooled my own children, I wanted to start studying foreign language with my children during freshman year. That gave me time, just in case something went wrong later on in high school. If I had trouble teaching or they had trouble learning French, I would still have an extra year of grace to start a different language.

Physical Education

While a physical education credit is not usually a requirement for college admission, it is still a good idea to spend some time on health and physical fitness in your homeschool. Encourage your child to engage in something physically active and then simply count credits. Count the hours your child spends skiing, swimming on the swim team, playing baseball, taking gymnastics classes, etc.

What about your couch potato? How do you get a couch potato to earn P.E. credit? Perhaps you could focus more on the education part of P.E. You could spend time teaching your child all about why fitness is important and you could also cover nutrition, first aid, and how to keep healthy. As part of their P.E. credit, your child could take self-defense classes, babysitting classes, or CPR and first aid classes.

Another idea for children who don't like traditional sports is dance. They can take dance classes or play computer dance games such as Dance Dance Revolution on the Wii. They may not even think of it as exercise because it's not an outside sport and it can be so much fun that it doesn't feel like work!

Fine Arts

The fine arts include music, visual arts, theater, and dance. Some homeschoolers dread the arts and others find themselves just swimming in art credits. When your child isn't fond of the arts, there are simple things you can do to get art credits. Consider a general class with an overview or survey of the various fine arts, incorporating a little bit of music, art, theater, and dance. Listen to music and learn about composers, visit art museums, attend live theater, and go swing dancing. If you have a book lover, go to the library and check out books on famous artists or read some Shakespeare plays.

I'm an art klutz myself. We worked hard to cover the fine arts in our homeschool. My children loved books, so I taught them a lot about fine arts through reading. At one point, I signed them up for a pottery class because I thought my boys would love playing with mud and it would just be perfect! I recorded it as a 6-week unit on fine arts, but they hated it. If you struggle with covering the fine arts as I did, your goal is to try to get in just one fine arts credit by the time your child graduates from high school.

If your child is already taking a music class of any kind, such as guitar lessons, piano lessons, or vocal lessons, then you already have the fine arts covered. You may be one of those families who work on fine arts all the time and don't even realize it. If your child already plays a musical instrument, is leading worship at church, or is involved in choir, you can add it to their fine arts credit.

When a child loves the fine arts, they might rack up quite a few high school credits. If they are involved in band, orchestra, and theater, they might get three credits of fine arts each year! When I was in public high school, I had friends who were in band, choir, and orchestra and they had three fine art credits every single year of high school. Over the four years, they accumulated 12 fine arts credits!

Chapter 4

Electives

Electives are any classes taken other than the core and beyond the basics, to provide the total of 22-24 high school credits required for graduation. Sometimes you can end up with so many electives! Your child can earn as many credits as you want. You don't have to graduate your child when they reach the usual 22-credit minimum.

There are three sources for electives. First are your state homeschool law requirements. Second are your family requirements. Third is the delight directed learning the student does for fun.

Always start with your state law requirements. Make sure you cover required electives and include them on your homemade transcript. In Washington State, for example, we are required to teach Occupational Education. It's easy to cover because you're probably already discussing careers as your child's guidance counselor. Teenagers will also want to learn about jobs and start working, which can become credit hours for Occupational Education class.

Consider an Occupational Education class even if you don't live in Washington State! At some point your child will be motivated by money to find a job. When they do, count work hours toward their class credit.

Family requirements vary, but they can also be a source of electives. Parents may require Bible each year, home economics, personal finance, auto-mechanics, critical thinking, logic or study skills. You are the guidance counselor and can decide what is best for your child.

Finally, electives might come from delight directed learning. Consider what your child loves to do. Take that interest and delight directed learning and include it in your transcript as an elective. If your child loves speech and debate, then that becomes an elective. It's not something required by state law, it's not something you have required of your children, it's just something they love doing. You're not force-feeding your child or giving them tests or worksheets; you simply follow behind them to scoop up their high school credits that occur naturally and include them on your homemade transcript.

Chapter 5

Create Great Homeschool Records

One of the core jobs for parents of a 9th or 10th grader is getting those homeschool records ready to go. When it comes to homeschool records, I find there are three types of moms. I call them Tubbies, Cubbies, and Binder Queens.

You might be one of the moms with a giant tub of information where you throw all of your homeschool paperwork. I call those moms Tubbies. In your tub in the schoolroom, you keep all of your child's work and homeschool records.

Perhaps you have a drawer full of information instead. I refer to these moms as Cubbies. It can be a bit more helpful if you have a drawer per child or a drawer per year. Often when you have more than one child, they will write similarly to each other because they all have the same penmanship teacher: you! Having a cubby or drawer for each child will help you keep it all straight, so you can remember who wrote each paper

You might be a bit more careful about your records and have everything contained in a binder or a folder. It has neat dividers, all divided up by subject. I call these super organized moms, Binder Queens.

Whether you're a Tubby, a Cubby, or a Binder Queen, it's important to work on your high school records every single year once your child reaches high school age. Use whichever record keeping system you have to gather what you need to create course descriptions and work on that transcript every year.

Homeschool Transcript

Your homeschool transcript is the official transcript for your child, so use the word "official" in the title with confidence. The transcript is a one-page, abbreviated overview of the high school years. It simply states the title of each class along with the grade and credit value. For instance, it would list Algebra 1 and that your child received an A and one credit. You might also like to include an abbreviated activity list right on the transcript. It could include things such as swim team, chess club, or Boy Scouts.

It's so important to work on your child's transcript every year because some summer camps and summer activities will require a high school transcript. If you want your child to go to a 9th grade science camp for example, they might need your transcript to confirm your child has taken algebra. When your child starts learning to drive in 10th grade, that homeschool transcript could earn your child a good student discount on car insurance. Make sure it's ready to go!

Working on your homeschool transcript every spring is a great habit to develop. Sometimes classes you intend to cover in the fall just don't pan out. You don't have to mention classes your child dropped on the transcript. By springtime, you know which classes fell through and which subjects replaced them. Get those transcripts up to date every spring.

Course Descriptions

Beyond the transcript, you also need to write course descriptions as part of your comprehensive homeschool record package to submit to colleges. Course descriptions don't have to be scary; they're simply very short paragraphs about what your child did in each class. List the details from the textbook table of contents.

You might also list what you used, for instance, Saxon Algebra 1 for math. If you went to the museum for the class or did some hands-on work, include it on your list. If for social studies class your child read a lot of historical fiction novels, list those readings along with the textbook or curriculum you used.

Finally, include information on how you graded the class in your course description. It can be a very simple explanation such as, "grade is determined by tests, quizzes, and hands-on report." You could also include more detail, such as "1/3 of the grade is from tests, 1/3 of the grade is based on quizzes, and 1/3 of the grade is based on daily work."

Limit your course descriptions to one page or less per class. The college admissions officer who reads your course descriptions isn't necessarily going to have the same love for the topic as you do; they just want information about each of the classes. You can make course descriptions less than a page, but never more.

Comprehensive Records

Comprehensive homeschool records begin with your transcript and course descriptions. Also of use to colleges are reading lists, an activity and awards list, and a work sample, such as an essay. Some homeschoolers also choose to include a resume.

When you're done with your comprehensive records, your child will look so smart and accomplished! It will look like everything in your homeschool went smoothly. Right now, you probably think that your homeschool would never look cool. It may always seem out of control and some curricula just never get finished. All that may be true, but when you get your child's accomplishments in black and white, it usually looks great!

Many homeschoolers who create comprehensive records have told me they not only earned great scholarships, but also found the process was such an encouragement! As homeschool moms, we are faced day to day with this intimate knowledge of our students and a crystal clear understanding of exactly what their failures are. It's difficult for us to see the bigger picture and where our children excel. As well as helping your child get into college and earn scholarships, keeping up with your records helps you feel better about your decision to homeschool and the achievements your child is making at home!

You can find free record keeping samples on The HomeScholar website, at:

www.TheHomeScholar.com/record-keeping-samples.php

You can also find all the tools, templates, and training needed to complete your homeschool records in the Total Transcript Solution and the Comprehensive Record Solution at:

www.TotalTranscriptSolution.com and www.ComprehensiveRecordSolution.com

Chapter 6

Take Important Tests

Don't panic about tests. Standardized tests and test preparation easily fit into your homeschool day. When your child is in 9th grade, the best preparation is to start with annual standardized tests. Many states will require a test each year, but if your state doesn't, I suggest you have your children take one anyway.

Annual testing can help in so many ways. It can help you determine what kind of grades you should give on the transcript. If you don't do a lot of testing in English class for instance, and you have your child reading or writing instead, standardized tests can help you decide which grade you should give them in that subject area.

It can also give your child practice with fill-in-the-bubble tests. When you take a standardized test, you take it with a group of homeschoolers or perhaps a hundred public school kids in a room. Sitting in a room full of kids, filling out sheets of standardized test bubbles for the very first time would be stressful to experience out of the blue in the final year of high school. Taking that annual standardized test will give your child some practice.

For your 9th grader, I encourage you to find a test at their grade level that you feel they will be successful in. Make sure your child will be successful so they don't feel like a failure. Early success will also help prevent test anxiety in future.

Consider having your child take the PLAN test in 9th or 10th grade. The PLAN is a pre-ACT test, just like the PSAT is a pre-SAT test. It's available in many schools across the US. In some states it's a bit harder to find. If you can't find a public school near you to take the PLAN test or you don't want your child to take it in a public school setting, look at tests such as the Iowa Basic, the ITBS, or the CAT.

There are many other standardized tests available. Check with your local homeschool group for other opportunities to take tests in a group setting.

Sometimes homeschoolers consider taking something like the SAT test early on. Keep in mind that the SAT test wasn't designed for your 9th grader; it's a college admission test designed for 11th graders. If your 9th grader takes a test written for 11th graders, they may feel completely overwhelmed! You want them to take a test they can be successful in, not something that will give them test anxiety and make them feel inferior. Stick with some sort of grade level test instead.

An annual standardized test is usually the first opportunity to practice filling in bubbles surrounded by strangers. I encourage you to have your child experience that in 9th grade. It will give you a sense of where your child is at compared to their peers and will give them some early practice for something they will have to do for college admission and as a college student.

High School Tests

The next step in high school testing is the PSAT. I encourage parents to have their children take the PSAT for fun in 10th grade. It's only offered once a year in October. Find out how to register in June of 9th grade or early September of 10th grade. It's usually as simple as calling your local high school to find out how your 10th grader can take the PSAT.

The PSAT is an inexpensive test - usually cheaper than an annual assessment. It's great practice for the SAT, but I encourage you to have your child take it for the first time in 10th grade. It's meant for 11th graders, but taking it in 10th grade usually isn't too much of a stretch. Since it's a much cheaper test, it makes a great first foray into the official college admission test situation.

The PSAT measures reading, writing, and math. You're most likely already covering these things with your child. You will be successful with the PSAT as long as those three subjects have been covered. Take time for a bit of practice with filling in the bubbles together first so they're prepared and don't freak out when they see them. It can be a little strange to read a question on a booklet and fill in the bubble to give your answer on a different piece of paper entirely.

There is an opportunity for a little practice before taking the PSAT. When you register for the test, you'll be given a sample booklet for practice at home. Take advantage of practice before they take the test in 10th grade at a public school.

After taking the PSAT or PLAN, your child will be all set for taking the SAT or ACT college admission tests. Decide in 10th grade which of those two tests is better for your child; they're two very different tests.

Statistically, one-third of kids will do better on the SAT, one-third will do better on the ACT, and one-third will do equally well on both. Choose the test that will make your child look smarter. Find a sample of each and give each sample test at home. Compare the scores to see which one gives your child a better score.

You probably don't need a sample of the SAT if your child has taken the PSAT because the PSAT gives you a practice score for the SAT. You only have to give a practice ACT at home and compare that score to the PSAT. Just add a zero to their PSAT score to determine their possible score on the SAT, as each subject area is graded between 200 and 800.

Each subject in the ACT is graded between 1 and 36 points. They don't exactly match up so look at the percentile...which one gives your child a higher percentile score? If they're in the 87th percentile for the SAT and they're in the 50th percentile for the ACT, you'll know that the SAT is the right test for them!

The SAT will always measure reading, writing, and math. As long as you teach those subjects, your child will be well prepared for the test. Prior to the test, have them study using test preparation books. Walk your child through a couple of sample tests before they take the test for real.

Test Preparation

Freshman Year

By far the best preparation at this stage is teaching children reading, writing, and math at their level. For math preparation, remember that the SAT and ACT include many algebra questions. It can be frustrating for teens to study with SAT or ACT tests before they have completed algebra. You don't want them to practice a test repeatedly that is filled with questions they simply can't answer correctly, because they haven't taken algebra yet.

For all children, the best preparation is to teach it at their level. A thorough understanding of Algebra 1 will give them a much better score on the SAT and the ACT than pushing them ahead too far too quickly.

For English test sections, vocabulary development is great test preparation. The SAT and the ACT involve vocabulary words, so make sure you include vocabulary in your studies. Read the article, "Play Your Way to a Great Vocabulary" for some fun vocabulary games you can start playing in your homeschool in 9th grade:

http://www.TheHomeScholar.com/
play-your-way-to-a-great-vocabulary.php

Penmanship is also important, because some major tests include hand-written essays. You want your child to be able to write reasonably fast and have legible handwriting. Penmanship style doesn't matter; what matters is that it's legible. The result you want is writing that any stranger could read (not as bad as a doctor's usually is). Usually students at the high school level will develop their own style of penmanship. You can encourage their own style just as long as it's legible.

Teaching general study skills can also help with test preparation. Practice timed tests. Using a study guide for a specific test can be part of a study skills class that you can include on the high school transcript.

Don't rush actual SAT practice with SAT booklets though. Remember the SAT is designed for 11th graders. You don't want to give them SAT questions that make them miss question after question. You don't want them to feel stupid by being exposed to all sorts of questions they can't possibly answer correctly.

Sophomore Year

Once you've decided between the SAT and the ACT, you want to start preparing with your child. For sophomore year, schedule test preparation for 30 minutes a day and use real sample tests. I often recommend Princeton Review study guides. These include real tests that have been used in the past.

These tests are all written by the same writers who will write them again in the future. The way they ask questions becomes very familiar with practice. Use these real sample tests about three times a week, giving them one 25-30 minute section at a time.

The SAT and the ACT measure reading, writing, and math. When you give them these sample tests, your child is practicing their reading, writing, and math and it becomes an assessment for you. You may not need to include a bunch of literary analysis, extra worksheets, math review, or grammar in your homeschool year, because they get it all as they study with these real sample tests!

I encourage you to practice a moderate amount of time each day and not to excess. Some experts suggest an hour a day every single day, even on weekends. I think that's more than most students need. Your child will get plenty of practice by working just half an hour, two to four times a week.

Chapter 7

Expect and Accept Gradual Maturity

Maturation of your teenager will occur slowly and gradually over time. Accept the fact that you can't speed up the process. Yes, what you're experiencing is normal and natural.

Maturation

You're going to see gradual changes. You will see increasing independence during freshman and sophomore year. That will also mean a gradual increase in the ability to self-teach. You may be in a hurry to get them teaching themselves, but it's a learned process that takes a while. They don't suddenly become organized overnight! Have patience.

When they do begin to teach themselves, that is not a failure on your part. That your child is teaching themselves doesn't mean you failed to teach chemistry, it means that you succeeded in raising an independent young adult. Your role has changed to become more of a mentor, or even a project manager.

In the midst of this maturation, and wanting your child to be more independent and more organized, you have to remember that life skills still have to be taught and not just caught. You can't expect them to see mom and dad get up at six in the morning and they will automatically get up at the same time; you have to explain why it's important in your home and gently encourage it.

Remember that the maturation process happens over years. Kids don't just wake up on the first day of 9th grade, decide to get up when their alarm clock goes off, and plan ahead to get their writing done by Friday. A reasonable expectation is to gradually see an increase in ability, organizational skills, responsibility, self-motivation, and direction. Their responsibility level will increase gradually with your help and with practice. Maybe they need to be given some consequences until it becomes a habit they will keep on their own.

Teenagers do have an increased sleep need...they require more sleep than adults and more sleep than even pre-teens. That can be frustrating because you're used to them getting up at a certain time and they seem lazy all of the sudden because they want to sleep all the time and don't get up easily. You do need to balance their sleep needs with the exhaustion they feel. I found that my teenagers seemed to function better when they were just a bit on the exhausted side of the scale; it seemed to keep their hormones in check. It is an observation you can explore to see if this is true for your own children.

Reasonable Expectations

Teach to mastery but do not expect perfection. It's like my checkbook: I have mastery over addition, subtraction, multiplication, and division, but my checkbook is not perfect and sometimes I will make mistakes. Give your teenagers natural consequences whenever you can rather than something extraordinary as a consequence; have a consequence decided in advance that is tied to the problem at hand.

Chapter 8

Technology Boundaries

It's a brave new world and with this comes new problems. Technological boundaries have become a problem for kids and adults alike. Teenagers especially have difficulty figuring out a technology balance, just as they have difficulty with any other life skill.

As parents and guidance counselors, we need to balance their online education with non-digital course work. I know one homeschool mom whose child's classes are all online. That is a very dangerous position for a kid to be in. If you add what they do for fun, they will be immersed in so much digital media that it can be overwhelming for them.

A lot of online education also works at a

set pace much like a public school classroom. It may not have built-in flexibility to develop delight directed learning and give your child free time to go outside. Balance any online education with non-digital coursework. At the same time, make sure your child knows how to use the computer and the internet. Balance is key.

Kids today tend to gravitate towards technology for every moment of free time they have, whether it's their smart phone or video games. You want to provide limitations so they have balance. Your hope is to teach them limits now so that when they leave the nest they will have learned good habits.

You want to make sure your boundaries include safety online. Monitor their free time. Make sure you are their Facebook friend, their Twitter follower, and their Instagram follower. Be your child's password holder so you can shut down their social media if they break safety rules or other established guidelines.

Technology Boundary Suggestions

Technology boundaries can be very difficult to set with young teens so discuss technology boundaries for your child with your spouse. You may want to consider a time limit on video games. In our homeschool, we set a daily limit of one hour for technology games of any kind.

Our children learned to set a time that they wanted to begin to play. If the timer was going, I knew how many minutes they had left. If the timer was not going, they could have been sitting there for hours and their time was obviously up for the day. That made it easy for us to manage as parents.

You might want to set a time limit for their online free time for each area: a time limit for playing games and one for time spent on Facebook or other social media. A specific time of day may work for you as well.

Studies actually show that having any digital media in the bedroom can interfere with sleep and cause sleep disorders. Not just for teenagers, but for adults, too. Your household rule may be no computers or technology in the bedroom: no phone, no iPad, and no computer that might be a temptation at night.

Teenagers may want to use their cellphones as an alarm clock in their room, but each time a friend texts they will answer it in the middle of the night! They could be awake for hours texting with friends. Many parents have a rule that phones and laptops have to be docked in the kitchen or the parents' room by a certain time every night.

Consider personal safety as well. Having unchecked use of a cell phone with a camera function may lead to some safety and security issues down the line. One stupid move could end up on the internet forever.

Set good boundaries that you as a family share together by not having technology at the dinner table. That means mom and dad aren't checking their phones either, which can be a challenge! You may also want to ban cell phones from the bathroom, which is a rule that will be appreciated by others, even if it isn't appreciated by your children!

Again, make sure that you as parents are Facebook friends with your child, that you possess all their passwords, and are following them on any social media. If they post something on Facebook or a picture on Instagram, you will see it. That will help them avoid making stupid decisions.

Important Technology Discussions

As your children mature, you can have serious discussions with them about technology. Internet addiction is a problem you need to discuss. Some young people become so enamored with technology that they start to require positive feedback online in order to feel good about their life. Without it, they feel depressed. Online gaming or other activities give them a shot of adrenaline, which makes them feel wonderful. You might want to do a bit of research together on the dangers of internet addiction with your teenager.

How do you know when it's become a problem? What are the key factors to look for? Ask yourself a few key questions. Are they able to get their schoolwork done? Do they have a life outside of technology? Will they go outside and play? Do they know how to play without technology? These are questions to ask when considering if your child has a problem with internet use.

Have a discussion about personal safety on the internet. Is your child giving out too much information online? Is the stranger they're chatting with a 15-year-old or is it a 40-year-old who's looking for somebody to prey on? You can also discuss how much information your child should give online about where they are, plans they're making, and when they're going away from home. Your child could be giving so much information out to the public. Hackers can even use information posted to get into bank accounts.

Probably more common than internet addiction or personal safety problems is future consequences of online behavior. There are consequences to what teens post online. You need to remind your children repeatedly that everything they post online is public and everything they post online is forever. Even when they delete it, even if it "disappears" from the screen, everything they post will be floating around in digital form forever. Somebody could track it down if they wanted to; even if you can't see it, somebody else knows how to get that information.

Share the consequences of posting inappropriately. Ask your child how they would feel if you as their mother posted something like that. If they take a selfie picture and think it's cute, but it's just slightly inappropriate, you could ask how they would feel if you took that selfie wearing that outfit. Employers check out social media and will be looking at these photos as part of the hiring process. Colleges look at social media as well; so will your child's future spouse. Make sure your child is informed.

Chapter 9

College Financing

Save Money

The easiest way to finance college is to simply start saving money early. Then spend some time during your homeschool years learning about college savings plans. Dave Ramsey has some great information on his website. Investigate the popular 529 Plans. You can also speak to your accountant or banker about how to save money for college. They can set you up with a budget and a plan.

It's also a good idea to teach your children the value of money. They can start earning and saving their own money for college. If they know they're required to chip in, they'll be more motivated to save.

Teaching your children the value of a dollar and giving them that strong work ethic can work well for them while they're in college.

Get Big Scholarships

The biggest scholarships actually come directly from colleges, so choose which colleges your child will apply to carefully. When you apply, you want to include colleges that are Reach, Fit, and Safety schools. If your child has an average SAT or ACT score, try to find a school that also has an average score for their incoming students; that's a Fit school. If a school tends to have a much higher average SAT or ACT score than your child's, that's a Reach school. If your test score is higher than the college's, then that is your Safety school.

Your child is going to apply to schools that are easy to get into, hard to get into, and medium hard to get into. That will give you the best chance of earning scholarships. Apply to at least 4 to 8 colleges and make sure there's a mix of public and private colleges.

Getting a higher SAT or ACT score can increase your child's chances of earning scholarships. Make sure your child maintains a high GPA as well, by teaching to mastery; not that their work is perfect, but that they understand before moving on.

You can also provide outside documentation, which will increase your chances of scholarship money. You might have your child take additional tests, such as subject tests. Your child can take some community college dual enrollment classes as well. They can seek great letters of recommendation from college professors. Comprehensive homeschool records with detailed course descriptions are also great documentation. These are all ways of clinching that big scholarship!

For more information on this topic, check out my Coffee Break Book, "Getting the BIG Scholarships."

Chapter 10

Career Exploration and Activities

Another extra for 9th and 10th grade is to spend time on career exploration. This will not only help your child decide which college to apply to, but also will help prepare your child for adult life.

Investigate Careers

You can investigate careers by having your child read books. There are books about careers and books which contain career aptitude tests. Have your child fill out assessment tools and personality tests to find out which careers they have an aptitude for. If your child attends college fairs, they could discuss with colleges what they enjoy doing and which careers their interests might suggest.

Your child might already be employed, even as a 9th or 10th grader. They could have jobs mowing the grass or baby-sitting. These jobs will help them in the process of deciding on a career for the future. They might decide that they like working outside, or decide that working with children is not for them.

Do not forget about being an entrepreneur. Your child can develop their own job as a student, making or selling something and developing a small business. You can go to www.MicroBusinessForTeens.com for some great information and resources.

Consider finding mentors that will help your child understand the subject they're passionate about. Mentors can be so inspirational and can help your child learn more about something they want to turn into a career for the future.

Activities and Leadership

Being engaged in activities is very helpful for finding friendships and giving your child a true enjoyment of learning. This can make homeschooling fun since your child can pursue their own interests.

Figure out what your child enjoys and this can turn into a meaningful activity. Meaningful activities, such as volunteering to teach chess to other children, may lead to leadership opportunities. Your child can become the teacher's assistant, either on a volunteer or paid basis.

Record these activities on their activities and awards list. Everything you add might lead to big scholarships. If your child is a leader, they can apply for scholarships in their area of leadership.

When your child doesn't seem to be interested in anything, then your job as the guidance counselor is to make sure your child experiments with different activities until they find something that they're passionate about. For example, one of my friends' sons experimented with different things like sports and music until he hit upon speech and debate. Speech and debate was his passion!

Successful Summertime

A successful summer should include a little bit of learning. Check out my college-bound reading list. Have your child read books on the list for pleasure over the summer. Don't forget to include them on your child's reading list.

www.TheHomeScholar.com/
college-bound-reading-list.php

You can also have your child pursue meaningful activities, especially if they are super busy during the school year. Summertime may be the only time they have to pursue extra-curricular activities. They may take on a summer job or do some volunteer service with church or Vacation Bible School. What they engage in over the summer can be included on their transcript as summer credits.

You can also add those summer activities to your activity list. If they're very involved with 4H during the summer, remember to put that on the activity list. Even if there is an activity you don't necessarily see as fun, if your child enjoys it then that will often help them find their passion.

Chapter 11

Looking Ahead to Sophomore Year

Foreign Language

Make sure you have started foreign language studies by the time your child is a sophomore. Colleges will require 2 to 4 years of foreign language. By starting in sophomore year, or earlier, you'll be where you need to be.

However, college is not the only reason to learn a language. Studying a foreign language will improve understanding of English grammar and vocabulary. It improves critical thinking skills because it takes effort and thought, and tends to increase a student's study skills.

Knowing a foreign language can improve your chances of employment. Many jobs in the marketplace give preference to a person who speaks a foreign language, including sales, construction, finance, and teaching. Learning a language can expand your worldview, and help you gain some cultural perspective. This can help a student learn more about the lifestyles and beliefs of people around the world, which can encourage reflection on why they believe and act the way they do. For Christians, language is an important component of The Great Commission. In Matthew 28, Jesus tells his disciples to "go and make disciples of all nations," which is much easier if you can speak the language of the country.

High School Tests

Have your child take the PSAT for fun in October of 10th grade. Register for the test in June of 9th grade or as late as September of 10th grade. The PSAT is the preliminary, practice, or pre-SAT. It's an important test, and great practice for the SAT as well as for the ACT. It can give you a good sense of what percentile your child is at compared to other children their age.

Each section is given a score of 20 to 80, with about 50 being an average score. When you get the results in December, add a zero to the score of each section, and that will estimate your child's score for the SAT. For example, if your child earns a 62 in the PSAT math section, it is likely they will get around 620 in math on the SAT.

When you get the score results, review what score range they are likely to have on the SAT, which will help you find a college that will match your academic rigor. The PSAT also provides practice taking standardized tests in what can be a rotten environment: in a sea of contagious diseases, surrounded by tattoos, body piercings, and smelly teenagers. Taking a timed test around strangers is difficult and it's more difficult when you haven't practiced it first. The PSAT can provide practice taking a test in "less than perfect" non-homeschooling conditions.

Sophomore year is when you decide between the two college admission tests: the SAT or the ACT. Have your child take a sample of each test and see which one your child gets a better score in. Once you have chosen between the SAT and ACT, have your child start studying for the test. I've seen statistics that claim boys do better on the SAT and girls do better on the ACT, but statistics do not always apply to your child. I've also heard that science lovers might do better on the ACT, and poor writers might do better on the ACT without the essay (although I recommend taking the essay).

What's MOST important is to decide which test is best for YOUR student. Taking a sample ACT and SAT is the best way to decide. While the sample test does take 3-4 hours (and it's a real pain, I know!), it can mean thousands of dollars in scholarship money, so it's worth the effort.

Consider whether a subject test is appropriate for your child. The AP Exams and SAT Subject Tests are required by some colleges, but not all. Choose which colleges your child might apply to, and the tests those colleges require for admission. If subject tests are required, make sure your child takes them in the spring.

Not all colleges require SAT Subject tests. Fewer still will require AP Exams. You only need to take the tests your college requires. Of course, the problem is knowing in advance which college your child may want to apply to at this early stage of high school.

If subject tests are necessary, it's a good idea to take a test in each general area of study: Math, English, History, Science, and Foreign Language. Your child should take subject tests after finishing the specific area being studied, so spring is the most common time for these tests. You can get more information from www.collegeboard.org.

Start thinking about which subject tests you might like your child to take: biology, French, or American history, for instance. Your child can take these through an SAT subject test, an AP class or AP exam, or a

CLEP exam. Those subject tests can help demonstrate proficiency in certain subjects. Sometimes colleges will want to see whether your child can demonstrate understanding in an area of math or their ability in science.

Beyond the Basics

There are little extras you can work on during sophomore year. You might want to do some research on dual enrolment in a community college for your child for future years. Keep in mind that community college can be a "Rated R" environment. Parents need to arm themselves with knowledge. Even when parents carefully choose the college curriculum and carefully select the teachers for their children, it is still an "adult" situation. Educate yourself about the pros and cons of community college, and then trust yourself to make a good decision that is the best for your child.

You might want to attend a college fair this year. Usually it's juniors who go, but I encourage sophomore students to go as well. Homeschoolers who live close to a large city should have an easy time finding a college fair nearby. If you search online for "college fair" and the name of your city, you will probably find several options.

In addition, there are larger fairs put on by private organizations each year. The biggest are the National Association for College Admission Counseling (nacacnet.org), and the North American Coalition for Christian Admissions Professionals (naccap.org).

There are also specialized groups that hold fairs. Exploring College Options Consortium represents Ivy League schools (exploringcollegeoptions.org), Colleges That Change Lives (ctcl.org), Historically Black Colleges and Universities (hbcufair.com) and Performing and Visual Arts fairs (nacacnet.org). If you feel like you're doing well, I encourage you to start finding a college in the spring of sophomore year.

Lee Binz, The HomeScholar

Chapter 12

Big Ideas for Success

Here are some big ideas that will help you start 9th and 10th grade well, then get all the way through, finish your classes, and be successful.

#1 Seek Balance and Sanity

One key to seeking balance is to put your weakest areas first. If you know your child's weak area is math, that's the first thing you should have them complete each day, it's the only thing you're not going to let go until they get it done.

Holding a morning meeting is also important. Have a meeting each day with your child to make sure they know you're keeping up with them and checking up on them. If you set your goal to have your morning meeting every single school day and only have it three days a week, that's three more days of accountability than they would have otherwise.

For me, coffee was the key to homeschool sanity. When I sat down with my coffee, I would have my morning meeting with my children. That's when I would also have my morning meeting with God. I would have my quiet time with my cup of coffee and my daily time of reflection.

When I was homeschooling, I had a friend who I met with for a cup of coffee almost every week to chat about the struggles we had, which was enormously helpful. It also gave me important time for margin and self-care; that was my way of taking care of myself so I would remain sane. It's important to have time set aside when you don't feel frantic!

#2 Remain Calm

There is nothing you can do with a 9th and 10th grader that would put you so far behind that you couldn't compensate in junior year. You have all sorts of freedom to mess up; even if things get bad, you can still fix it come junior year. Start strong and do your best. At the same time, don't double up or be obsessive in your efforts to catch up because your child is behind!

Choose curriculum that fits the student because your child is working towards self-teaching. It becomes less important that the curriculum fits you, because you're starting to fade into the background.

The difficulties that you face shall pass. This is a season of your life and, thankfully, not a life sentence! It will get better because your children will grow up.

#3 Encourage Delight Directed Learning

Once your child is in high school, it's even more important to encourage delight directed learning. Encourage what they're passionate about and what do they do for fun? Whatever they do for fun is usually something you can encourage. Look closely at what annoys you because it's often something they find fun! Whenever I asked my children to make their bed or empty the dishwasher, they usually did something much more fun instead. Pay attention! Often that will help you figure out what their passion is.

Once you find delight directed learning for them, make sure you include those high school credits on their transcript. At the same time you want to avoid turning their delight directed learning into schoolwork by making worksheets or tests about something they enjoy doing. Follow behind and scoop up all the high school credits. Don't turn delight into drudgery.

#4 Take Continuing Education Classes

Learn more about homeschooling high school. There's always something you can learn. Don't panic; just take it a little at a time. My Gold Care Club online classes are arranged in Quick Start, Beginner, Intermediate, Advanced, and Encouragement sections so you can find the class that will be helpful, no matter how much you know about homeschooling high school. The Gold Care Club has new classes available every month along with a monthly live webinar with live question and answer time. You can find out more about the Gold Care Club here:

www.TheHomeScholar.com/gold-care.php

Try to get to a homeschool convention and take classes there if possible. Get the continuing education you need! If you don't have access to a homeschool convention that discusses high school specifically, try out my Convention at Home Kit.

http://www.thehomescholar.com/convention-at-home-kit.php

Suggested Resources

If you're looking for some resources and trying to start out right with a 9th or 10th grader, I suggest reading my book, "Setting the Records Straight: How to Craft Homeschool Transcripts and Course Descriptions for College Admission and Scholarships." Get help with creating the comprehensive records you need for college admission and perfectly document the amazing homeschool education you're providing for your child!

You may also enjoy my Coffee Break Book, "Planning High School Courses" to help you plan out the four years of high school right from the start.

Appendix 1

The Best Guidance Counselor is YOU!

I have read that a public high school guidance counselor helps, on average, 315 students. That's three hundred fifteen young adults to one adult. Consider how many students there are in your high school. You could have probably up to four high school students at a time. Which school do you believe has the better student-to-advisor ratio? Take into account the simple fact that you actually LOVE your child, and that you are sentimentally and financially invested in their lasting success. Despite the fact that you might be only half as good as a public high school guidance counselor, you are able to be hundreds of times more effective.

While getting my hair cut, I overheard a conversation between two mothers of high school teens. They were talking about how they had moved their children from public schools and private schools, looking for an excellent education and yet unable to find it. "They just don't teach the basics of reading, writing and math anymore!" one mother moaned. The other mom explained, "And my child is getting entirely lost in the system!" She went on to summarize how her child completed Algebra 1 with difficulty. The following year, the guidance counselor signed her child up for the wrong class. This poor student was sitting in a calculus class for TWO WEEKS before anyone found out that he wasn't supposed to be there!

I understand that homeschoolers often feel inferior about their capability to counsel their children in high school. You have to admit, however, that a homeschooler would NEVER stick their child in a Calculus class after having difficulties with Algebra 1! We might not be excellent high school advisors, but we do definitely KNOW our child, and that's what makes us successful!

Pop Quiz!

Take this short quiz to see how you measure up against the other guidance counselors. The US Department of Education reports that 92% of high school guidance counselors do five important tasks.

1. Use College Catalogs

These substantial catalogs resemble gigantic phone books, and they are found in public libraries. If you know where your public library is OR you know how to buy books online, give yourself one point.

2. Individual Counseling Sessions

Have you spoken to your teenager recently? Would you consider that an individualized conversation? If so, give yourself one point. I know that in various high schools, guidance counselors ask that a student bring a list of their activities or a resume with them when they meet. If you had to ask your child to bring a resume to your individual counseling session, subtract one point.

3. Use of online career information resources

Homeschoolers who don't have computers in their homes can use the computer at a library or resource center. If a computer is not available, a librarian can direct you to career information sources in print. If you know where your public library is OR you know how to make use of a computer, give yourself one point.

4. Put together and interpret tests for career planning

Two websites offer you all the high school tests. One is collegeboard.com and the other is ACT.org. Once you know about those two websites, you will have all the information you need to schedule and understand high school tests. If you can locate these websites on the internet, give yourself one point.

5. Make use of offline career information sources

If you have spoken to your child about getting a job, if your child has ever earned money in any way or held a non-paying job of any kind, or if you know how to make use of your public library, give yourself one point.

How did you score? If you received 5 points, you are offering the same service as a public school guidance counselor. Less than 5 points may warrant some kind of remedial computer services. Just ask your teen for help; you'll be up to speed in no time!

Focus on Flexibility

Teenagers will change their minds, so you need to focus on being flexible. College preparation makes a whole lot of sense for students who plan on going to college. College-bound students will need course work designed to prepare them for their college studies. Students will need to take college admission tests and parents will need to learn about grades and credits. College-bound students need a homeschool diploma and a homeschool transcript. College preparation for college bound students is expected.

Have you ever taken into consideration what a college preparatory home education might offer for students who will not go to college? Rigorous academics could benefit children even though they are not planning for higher education. Without college, a homeschool education could very well be the only formal education a student will be given.

Academic preparation can't hurt! Plan for college and give rigorous high school academics. If they use it to go to college, that's fantastic! If they don't use it for college, does the hard work go to waste? By no means! College preparation may help your child be a more effective employee or business owner, a smarter citizen and a more self-confident homeschool parent. Planning for college can't hurt your child, and it will be able to deliver flexibility for the future.

Project Management 101

College preparation necessitates that you take a "project manager" role. Homeschool parents assume four main roles throughout their children's lives: caretaker, teacher, mentor and friend. During high school, the teacher role becomes less and less important. Our job gets to be more administrative, however it is not going to become more time-consuming or more complicated; it's simply different.

Plan Courses

Plan your high school classes. Throughout eighth and ninth grade, find out about your own state requirements and try to make a system to meet those requirements. Look at the common college expectations for recommended high school courses. Look over your high school plan yearly and adjust your plan. Budding nurses and engineers might have to buckle down with math, and those getting ready to be missionaries could possibly benefit from additional foreign languages.

Plan for Tests

Arrange for standard high school tests. What tests do you take, when do you take them, and how do you know? The vast majority of those answers are found on two websites: CollegeBoard.com and ACT.org. Take the PSAT in 10th grade for fun, and in 11th grade to be considered for the National Merit Scholarship. The SAT and ACT are typically taken in spring of 11th grade and repeated senior year only if necessary. Subject tests are best taken immediately after you finish each subject and might be required by some colleges

Find Extracurricular Activities

You desire your kids to be well rounded, and so do colleges. Encourage your child to volunteer or seek employment, internships or apprenticeships. Encourage activities like sports, music, art, and other experiences. Colleges love to see kids who are enthusiastic about something. They can see this elusive "passion" in extra-curricular activities that students maintain through all four years of high school.

Find a College

To accomplish your intention of selecting ideal colleges, the first step is to go to a college fair. Comparable to a homeschool convention, it's a fast and straightforward way to learn a lot about quite a few colleges in a brief amount of time. Step two is taking the PSAT in October of junior year. Step three is taking time to stop by colleges during the year, so you can eliminate poor choices from your list. The fourth step is taking the SAT or ACT in the spring, which might help you discover the appropriate college fit academically and financially.

Contemplate College Finances

We all know we "should" be saving for college, however I realize intentions don't always match reality. Regardless of your savings success, don't be afraid to look at private colleges. They sometimes provide considerably better financial aid than public schools, and usually their costs are comparable to state schools.

College tuition is like buying a car. Hardly anyone pays the sticker price so don't be afraid of the list price of a school. In January of senior year, parents need to complete the FAFSA. The Free Application for Federal Student Aid is an IRS-style form which will decide how much money the government believes you will be able to afford to pay for college, usually with comical results! Here we are, worrying about the price of gasoline, and they think we can manage that amount? The FAFSA may also be used to find out how much financial aid colleges will give you.

Prepare High School Records

When you determine which colleges your child will apply to, ask those colleges what high school records they need from you. It could vary drastically, and there is no way to know unless you ask. They could request only a transcript. Some colleges could also want a simple reading list, but others will want exhaustive course descriptions and grading criteria. Some colleges will have very unusual and unique requirements. Find out their requirements early on to make sure you can give them what they need.

That's why I always advise keeping everything in the high school years, because you never know what they will want. One college asked me for an English paper that I had graded. Another college needed subject tests in several different areas. Like a boy scout, always be prepared! At the very end of homeschooling, at the end of senior year, don't forget to send the college a final transcript that includes graduation date, final grades and grade point average.

Apply to College

Guide the college application process. College applications are generally lengthy and complex. Admission essays will be tedious and time consuming. Plan to begin the application process during September of senior year to allow a sufficient amount of time to complete it in a timely fashion. It's possible to write college application essays in junior year if you prefer to plan ahead. You can always alter it again before submitting.

Begin Early

Each college may require two or more essays, and their application could be many more extra pages. Quite often, admission and financial aid decisions are "first come, first served" which means it can definitely be worthwhile to plan ahead. I encourage students to finish applications by January first whenever possible, to be in the best possible situation. The college deadline might be later, but they are going to be overloaded with applicants near the deadline. They can give your application a more relaxed reading if you turn it in early.

Keep it Simple!

You have only one goal per year in the four years of high school. During freshman year, all you have to do is contemplate college. Sophomore year is the time to prepare yourself for college. The focal point of junior year is selecting a few colleges where you would like to apply. During senior year, the main goal is completing college applications.

Be Confident in the Benefits of Homeschooling

Homeschoolers have the advantage in college preparation! We are intimately involved in the education of our children. We truly recognize their strengths and weak points, their ambitions and passions. We can offer the best guidance counseling for them because we are love-givers, not just caregivers. In school settings, a guidance counselor may know a lot about tests and deadlines, that's true. They have hundreds of students to guide, and they might speak to each student only once or twice. Just like our fantastic student-teacher ratio, our student-advisor ratio just can't be beat!

The guidance counselor at a public school has a huge job. They are responsible for the college and career plans of hundreds of kids they don't know. Our job as homeschool parents is significantly more manageable. We are only responsible for our own children; children we know extremely well.

Be brave! Parents know their child better than anyone, and they are completely capable of offering the guidance they require through high school. You can do it!

As a wise sage said, "Remember, amateurs built the ark. Professionals built the Titanic."

Afterword

Who is Lee Binz, and What Can She Do for Me?

Number one best-selling homeschool author, Lee Binz is The HomeScholar. Her mission is "helping parents homeschool high school." Lee and her husband Matt homeschooled their two boys, Kevin and Alex, from elementary through high school.

Upon graduation, both boys received four-year, full tuition scholarships from their first choice university. This enables Lee to pursue her dream job - helping parents homeschool their children through high school.

On The HomeScholar website, you'll find great products for creating homeschool transcripts and comprehensive records to help you amaze and impress colleges.

Find out why Andrew Pudewa, Director at Institute for Excellence in Writing says: "Lee Binz knows how to navigate this often confusing and frustrating labyrinth better than anyone."

You can find Lee online at:

www.TheHomeScholar.com

If this book has been helpful, could you please take a minute to write us a quick review on Amazon?

Thank you!

Testimonials

Thank You for the Gold Care Club

Dear Lee,

Thank you so much! I have incorporated all of your great ideas. I also wanted to let you know how much I appreciate the Gold Club and how you have helped me keep focused. Last Friday, at our Friday school co-op I shared with some high school homeschooling moms how happy I am with your service and help, and they are considering joining.

I tell everyone I know about how you are helping me, because you truly are a gift from God. Because this homeschool high school college prep is scary! I also tell about your website and your products, so I am hoping you are getting some new customers purchasing your products.

Blessings,
Susanne

Scholarship to Pepperdine!

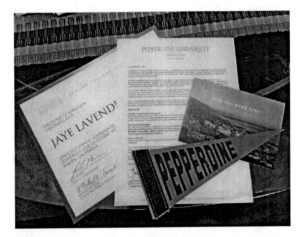

Dear Lee,

I just had to write to let you know that my daughter received the Regent's Scholarship for Pepperdine University! This is a $40,700 annual award. I am still in shock daily. We found out a week ago, and it has taken this long for it to actually sink in.

Of course this is after hours and hours of work on both of our parts, my daughter writing countless essays and filling out applications, and me writing course descriptions. But we figured out that even if we spent 100 hours in the process, we were actually making about $1600 an hour!

I cannot thank you enough for all the direction you have given me over the past few years. Honestly, the college application process has proven to be one of the most challenging things I have ever done. It challenged my faith and sanity. I cannot imagine trying to do it on my own.

Thank you for choosing to spend your post-schooling years helping others! The prospect of home schooling high school IS scary, but looking back, the blessing of intimacy I now share with my daughter by having spent these past four years together was worth it. Thank you for helping me to feel the fear and do it anyway!

Sincerely,
Traci Minor

For more information about my **Gold Care Club**, go to:

www.TheHomeScholar.com/gold-care.php

Also From The HomeScholar...

- The HomeScholar Guide to College Admission and Scholarships: Homeschool Secrets to Getting Ready, Getting In and Getting Paid (Book and Kindle Book)
- Setting the Records Straight - How to Craft Homeschool Transcripts and Course Descriptions for College Admission and Scholarships (Book and Kindle Book)
- Preparing to Homeschool High School (DVD)
- Finding a College (DVD)
- The Easy Truth About Homeschool Transcripts (Kindle Book)
- Parent Training A la Carte (Online Training)

- Total Transcript Solution (Online Training, Tools and Templates)
- Comprehensive Record Solution (Online Training, Tools and Templates)
- Gold Care Club (Comprehensive Online Support and Training)
- Homeschool "Convention at Home" Kit (Book, DVDs and Audios)

The HomeScholar "Coffee Break Books" Released or Coming Soon on Kindle and Paperback:

- Delight Directed Learning: Guiding Your Homeschooler Toward Passionate Learning
- Creating Transcripts for Your Unique Child: Help Your Homeschool Graduate Stand Out from the Crowd
- Beyond Academics: Preparation for College and for Life
- Planning High School Courses: Charting the Course Toward High School Graduation
- Graduate Your Homeschooler in Style: Make Your Homeschool Graduation Memorable
- Keys to High School Success: Get Your Homeschool High School Started Right!

- Getting the Most Out of Your Homeschool This Summer: Learning just for the Fun of it!
- Finding a College: A Homeschooler's Guide to Finding a Perfect Fit
- College Scholarships for High School Credit: Learn and Earn With This Two-for-One Strategy!
- College Admission Policies Demystified: Understanding Homeschool Requirements for Getting In
- A Higher Calling: Homeschooling High School for Harried Husbands (by Matt Binz, Mr. HomeScholar)
- Gifted Education Strategies for Every Child: Homeschool Secrets for Success
- College Application Essays: A Primer for Parents
- Creating Homeschool Balance: Find Harmony Between Type A and Type Zzz...
- Homeschooling the Holidays: Sanity Saving Strategies and Gift Giving Ideas
- Your Goals this Year: A Year by Year Guide to Homeschooling High School
- Making the Grades: A Grouch-Free Guide to Homeschool Grading
- High School Testing: Knowledge That Saves Money

- Getting the BIG Scholarships: Learn Expert Secrets for Winning College Cash!
- Easy English for Simple Homeschooling: How to Teach, Assess and Document High School English
- Scheduling - The Secret to Homeschool Sanity: Plan You Way Back to Mental Health
- Junior Year is the Key to High School Success: How to Unlock the Gate to Graduation and Beyond
- Upper Echelon Education: How to Gain Admission to Elite Universities
- How to Homeschool College: Save Time, Reduce Stress and Eliminate Debt
- Homeschool Curriculum That's Effective and Fun: Avoid the Crummy Curriculum Hall of Shame!
- Comprehensive Homeschool Records: Put Your Best Foot Forward to Win College Admission and Scholarships
- Options After High School: Steps to Success for College or Career
- How to Homeschool 9th and 10th Grade: Simple Steps for Starting Strong!

- Senior Year Step-by-Step: Simple Instructions for Busy Homeschool Parents

Would you like to be notified when we offer the next *Coffee Break Books* free or discounted during our Kindle promotion days? Leave your name and email below and we will send you a reminder.

http://www.TheHomeScholar.com/freekindlebook.php

Visit my Amazon Author Page!

amazon.com/author/leebinz

CPSIA information can be obtained
at www.ICGtesting.com
Printed in the USA
FFOW04n1318120117
31305FF